TOOLS FOR CAREGIVERS

- **F&P LEVEL:** C
- **WORD COUNT:** 23
- **CURRICULUM CONNECTIONS:** holidays, traditions

Skills to Teach

- **HIGH-FREQUENCY WORDS:** get, see, we
- **CONTENT WORDS:** cards, gifts, give, hearts, love, make, show
- **PUNCTUATION:** exclamation point, periods
- **WORD STUDY:** long /e/, spelled ee (*see*); long /o/, spelled ow (*show*); short /i/, spelled i (*gifts, give*)
- **TEXT TYPE:** factual description

Before Reading Activities

- Read the title and give a simple statement of the main idea.
- Have students "walk" through the book and talk about what they see in the pictures.
- Introduce new vocabulary by having students predict the first letter and locate the word in the text.
- Discuss any unfamiliar concepts that are in the text.

After Reading Activities

Explain to readers that Valentine's Day is a day to show love. Flip back through the book as a group. In what ways do people in the book show love? Who do they show love to? Ask readers how they show love to the people close to them.

Tadpole Books are published by Jump!, 5357 Penn Avenue South, Minneapolis, MN 55419, www.jumplibrary.com

Copyright ©2022 Jump! International copyright reserved in all countries. No part of this book may be reproduced in any form without written permission from the publisher.

Editor: Jenna Gleisner **Designer:** Molly Ballanger

Photo Credits: Maglara/Shutterstock, cover; khz/Shutterstock, 1; Monstar Studio/Shutterstock, 2mr, 3; Oksana_Slepko/Shutterstock, 2tl, 2br, 4–5; Chih Yuan Wu/Dreamstime, 6–7; Gelpi/Shutterstock, 2ml, 8–9; Jose Luis Pelaez Inc/Getty, 2tr, 10–11; siro46/Shutterstock, 12; ViewStock/Shutterstock, 13; AJ_Watt/iStock, 2bl, 14–15; kirin_photo/iStock, 16.

Library of Congress Cataloging-in-Publication Data
Names: Zimmerman, Adeline J., author.
Title: Valentine's Day / by Adeline J. Zimmerman.
Description: Minneapolis, Minn.: Jump!, Inc., 2022. | Series: Holiday fun! | Includes index. | Audience: Ages 3–6
Identifiers: LCCN 2020047551 (print) | LCCN 2020047552 (ebook) | ISBN 9781636900995 (hardcover)
ISBN 9781636901008 (paperback) | ISBN 9781636901015 (ebook)
Subjects: LCSH: Valentine's Day—Juvenile literature.
Classification: LCC GT4925 .Z56 2022 (print) | LCC GT4925 (ebook) | DDC 394.2618—dc23
LC record available at https://lccn.loc.gov/2020047551
LC ebook record available at https://lccn.loc.gov/2020047552

HOLIDAY FUN!

VALENTINE'S DAY

by Adeline J. Zimmerman

TABLE OF CONTENTS

Words to Know	2
Valentine's Day	3
Let's Review!	16
Index	16

WORDS TO KNOW

cards

gifts

give

hearts

love

make

VALENTINE'S DAY

heart

We make hearts.

card

We make cards.

We give cards.

flowers

We give gifts.

We show love.

LET'S REVIEW!

Valentine's Day is on February 14. It is a holiday that celebrates love. How is this family celebrating?

INDEX

cards 5, 7
gifts 9, 11
give 7, 9

hearts 3
love 13, 15
show 15